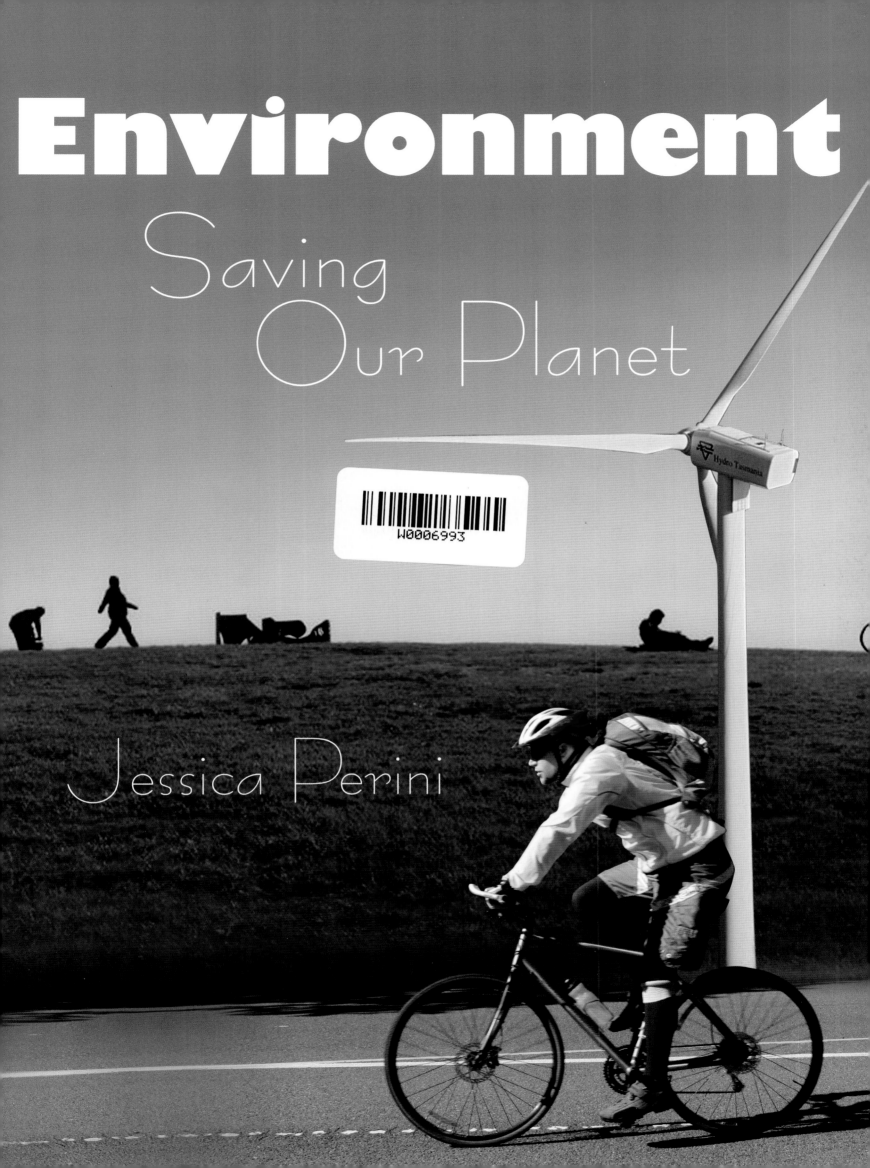

Environment

Saving Our Planet

Jessica Perini

Contents

Exploring the
Environment

Is there anything more beautiful than the Earth? Think about it for a second. This planet is just the right distance from the sun. It is the only planet in our solar system known to have liquid water. It has a thin atmosphere that helps us breathe. But sometimes, humans can throw nature's systems out of balance. They do this by polluting the Earth and in many other ways. So our job is to do the best we can to protect this lovely planet. After all, it's the only Earth we have!

What is the Environment?

Look around you. The environment is everywhere. Trees, flowers, birds, tiny ants, oceans and lakes are all part of our natural environment. Look again, and you will notice buildings, cars and machines. These also make up the environment. The environment is also about what we can't see, like the air.

Water is Life: Don't Waste a Drop

Of all the planets in our Solar System, Earth is the only one known to have liquid water. This comes in the form of oceans, seas, rivers and lakes, which provide food, minerals, medicines, building products, places to live, water to drink, petrol and shipping routes. The Sun beats down on the ocean, which absorbs the heat. The ocean sends the heat around the world to your place and mine. Oceans also lock away lots of **carbon dioxide**, one of the **greenhouse gases** that causes **global warming**.

The Air We Breathe

If you hold your breath your face wil turn blue and you'll feel light-headed. Breathing is something we do thousands of times a day, so we sometimes take it for granted. But it is just as important to humans, animals and plants as food and water. So when we pollute our air with smoke from cars, industry and farming we are putting ourselves and our plants and animals in great danger.

Eco-friendly, Ecosystems and Ecology

If you go to a supermarket you'll see a lot of products with the word 'eco' on them. 'Eco' comes from a Greek word that means 'house'. So often when 'eco' is used it means the environment we live in. 'Ecosystem' means a community of plants and animals and how they work together. Like how coral in a reef need fish for their survival. 'Ecology' is the study of how things rely on each other to survive.

Earth Under Our Feet

Land is the area on Earth not covered by water, making up 30 per cent of the Earth. Humans use land to build houses and farm crops (like corn and wheat) and animals (like cows and chickens). We also dig up minerals like coal, which helps heat our homes and run our cars. But land is important for all types of plants and animals. It provides lots of **ecosystems**—homes for animals and plants. If we wipe out forests to create more farms, or when we mine the Earth, we can damage these precious ecosystems.

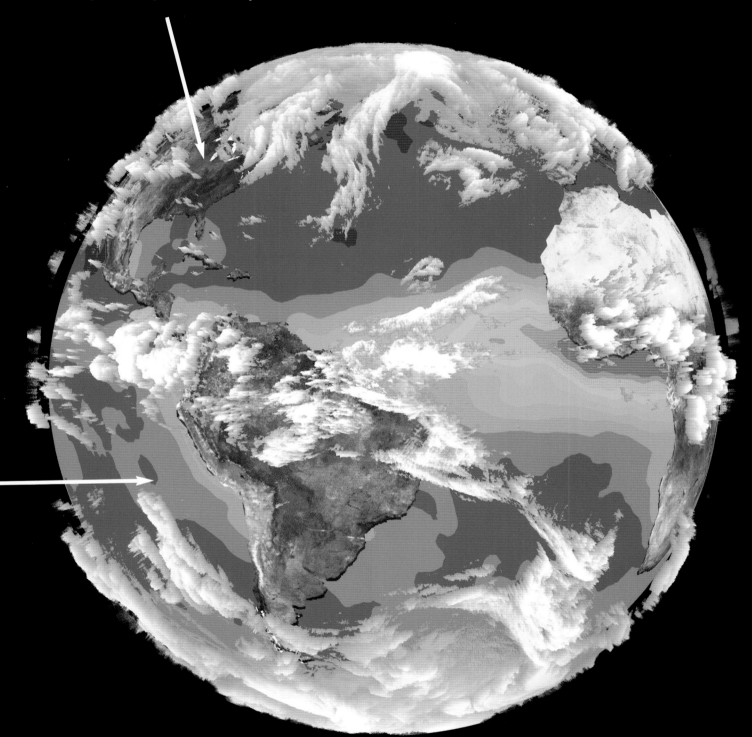

Saving the Planet

Pollution in the air and water and hotter weather than normal are just a few signs that the Earth is sick. Humans and animals need fresh air, clean running water and trees to survive. So do animals and plants. We need to care for our environment. People working to do just that are called 'environmentalists' and this book will help show you how to be an environmentalist too.

Mind-boggling Biodiversity

Life on Earth is like one big family; each part is linked to another. A tree produces air that animals can breathe. Animals breathe out air that plants need to survive. Leaves fall to the forest floor and are eaten by creatures. Their poo becomes soil. In that soil another tree grows. A similar process occurs in the ocean, where plants and **algae** feed a multitude of marine life and fish feed on each other. Animals, plants, fungi and bugs are all part of this great **biodiversity**. Biodiversity is the great circle of life on Earth: all the creatures and plants and other systems that rely on each other to survive. These food chains are called **ecosystems** and if you take any part of that system out, the system will break down.

Amazing Animals

Animals provide food for other animals and fertiliser (their poo) for plants. They work for humans too. Guide dogs help blind people, and horses transport people from one place to another. Some animals, like dogs and cats, have been domesticated and make great companions. Animals are an essential part of food chains, so ensuring their survival is very important to the environment. People often build their own homes wherever animals live and breed. But if humans take up too much space, animals either have to move or they starve.

Precious Plants

Plants produce oxygen so that other living things can breathe. They provide water, clothing, shelter and building materials. People use plants as medicine, to kill germs and as painkillers. Plants are at the beginning of the food chain—they take minerals and gases from the environment and pass them on to animals that eat them. So, as you can see, life without plants simply wouldn't be worth living!

Food Chains and Apex Predators

Humans, animals and plants are all part of a massive 'food chain'. An example of a food chain is:

Poo of snails, small fish,
large fish and sharks feeds the plankton

Shark eats the large fish

Snail eats plankton

Large fish eats the small fish

Small fish eats the snail

Those on the top of the food chain are called 'apex predators'. These include sharks and humans. Apex predators are normally not eaten by anything else, although humans do tend to eat anything including other apex predators! If you take apex predators out of the food chain, other parts of the chain can break down. For example, Tiger Sharks in Shark Bay, Western Australia, eat green sea turtles and dugong. The turtles and dugong feed on the sea grass in this region. If the sharks disappeared then the turtles and dugong might eat all the grass and then starve. So by wiping out sharks, you'd endanger an entire ecosystem.

Beneficial Bugs

Bugs provide food for animals and plants. They **pollinate** plants, helping them make fruits. Beneficial bugs, like the ladybeetle, help keep other insect populations under control. Most insects break down plants into good fertile soil. They also burrow into soil, introducing air and water, which helps plants grow.

Bees not only make honey, they also pollinate plants. This helps many crops we rely on for food to produce fruit.

Fabulous Fungi

Mushrooms and toadstools are fungi. They break down plants, creating soil and food for plants and animals. Some ants, termites and beetles eat fungi. Humans depend on fungi too, as some fungi help make foods and drinks, like smelly blue vein cheese and wine. Fungi have been used to create **antibiotics** that save millions of human lives. Some fungicides (chemicals that kill fungi) can be toxic to humans, animals and plants, as well as fungi.

9

Earth out of Balance

Earth's oceans contain extraordinary marine life and the land is home to millions of varieties of insects, plants and animals. But humans (especially in richer countries like ours) are using up these resources faster than they are being replaced. We are also polluting the environment. But it's not too late. We can all help to fix the environment. We can start by living a **sustainable** life. This means not making things we don't need, and recycling as much as we can.

Sharing Resources

There are about 6.5 billion people in the world. About half have little access to medicine, electricity, safe water and reliable food supplies. Richer countries need to use less of everything, including fossil fuels, farm land, minerals, wood, metals and marine life. This can be done by encouraging smarter shopping, recycling and less use of chemicals. Poorer countries need better health care, food, resources, technology and education. Resources need to be shared fairly and wisely.

The world's population continues to grow: in 1820 it reached 1 billion people, by 2000 it was 6 billion. Will the Earth be able to continue to support the human race? Not until we get smart about the environment!

Pollution and its Effects

This cyclist wears a face mask to avoid breathing in air pollution.

The more people there are on the Earth, the more waste there is. Chemicals spill out into the air, water and land. This threatens **ecosystems** and our health and damages the planet. An increase in greenhouse gases in the atmosphere is causing the Earth to heat up. This is called **global warming**. Some people argue that we can simply do without many of the products that create the pollution in the first place. Others say we can replace harmful chemicals with ones that are **biodegradable** (that is they easily break down into harmless things).

Resources Running Low

The Earth's resources can be broken up into two categories: renewable and non-renewable. Renewable resources are things that can be re-grown, or that will last the Earth's lifetime. They include food, forests and solar and wind power. Non-renewable things are those that will run out, like coal, petroleum and natural gas. Humans are using up non-renewable resources very quickly. Within the next 100 years many of these things will run out. We need to start using renewable resources and use them more wisely.

This lonely tree was all that was left of a lush hill in this area of Davao City, Philippines, after developers moved in. A week later the tree was gone.

Extinctions

Using up the world's resources destroys **ecosystems**. We tear down rainforests to create farms, heat houses and build furniture, taking away places where animals live or polluting their habitats. Some animal and plant species become extinct and many species are endangered. Others are forced into new areas. Extinction is a natural part of life. But the Earth's animals are becoming extinct faster than any other time in history.

Boyd's Forest Dragon is threatened with extinction due to climate change.

Ice Reveals Warming

We can see evidence of warming in many of the Earth's systems. For example we can measure land and ocean temperatures. You can take samples from the ocean, lakes, trees, coral and air. But how do you know how hot the air was when mammoths roamed the Earth? You can see it in the ice! We know this because tiny bubbles of ancient air were trapped in layers of ice. In places like Antarctica scientists drill under the surface of the ice. By taking out what's called an 'ice core' scientists can get an idea of what the air was like in the past.

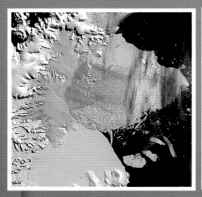  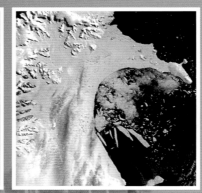 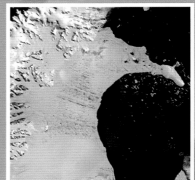

One dramatic event took place in Antarctica in early 2002. Antarctica's Larsen Ice Shelf lost an area larger than the Australian Capital Territory in 31 days!

Mega Melt

During the last few years many of the Earth's glaciers and ice sheets have been melting. Less ice means less sun is reflected and there is more warming. Also loss of the ice shelves allows the glaciers draining Antarctica to flow faster, causing sea levels to rise faster.

Venice is famous for its gondolas. But the Italian city is sinking as the water levels rise.

Effects of Climate Change

An increase in the temperature of the Earth would lead to massive changes on land and in the ocean. Natural ecosystems would change as animals become **extinct** or move to new habitats. Sea creatures would be affected by changes in the ocean's saltiness. But humans would be affected too. Crops would be difficult to grow without enough water and some people would even have to leave their homes if sea levels rise. Climate change would also cause extreme storms and flooding in some areas.

Hurricanes such as Hurricane Katrina, which occurred in America in 2006, would increase due to global warming.

Climate Change

Climate refers to the weather in a region: how hot it is, how much rain falls or how windy it gets. **Climate change** means a big change in those weather patterns. Scientists tell us that the Earth has warmed over the last 50 years and that humans are most likely the cause. Our cities, cars, industry pollution and destruction of forests for farming add to global warming. **Global warming** is a rise in the Earth's temperature. It could lead to climate change, causing floods, droughts and severe storms. Sea levels could rise as land ice melts and sea water expands.

The Greenhouse Effect

Think of our Earth as a huge **greenhouse**. Most of the time it stays nice and warm due to greenhouse gases (like methane, carbon dioxide, ozone and nitrous oxide) in the **atmosphere** that trap heat; this is called the greenhouse effect. Greenhouse gases are released naturally when plants break down and animals digest food. But recently scientists have found a lot more of these gases in the Earth's our atmosphere and believe this is due to human activity. Too much of these gases means the planet is getting hotter, causing global warming.

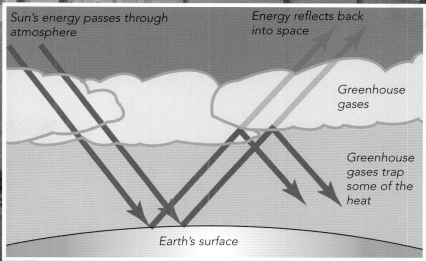

Sun's energy passes through atmosphere

Energy reflects back into space

Greenhouse gases

Greenhouse gases trap some of the heat

Earth's surface

This diagram shows how the greenhouse effect works.

What Can We Do About Climate Change Today?

The Earth's atmosphere may get better over the next few hundred years. But we need to stop damaging it really soon. If we wait too long we may not be able to undo the harm. World leaders need to join together to fight global warming. But you and I can also do our bit. The list below shows ways we can lessen **greenhouse gases**.

✳ Plant trees ✳ Buy less wood ✳ Use wind and solar power ✳ Use your feet, bike or bus rather than a car ✳ Eat more veggies and less meat ✳ Use natural heating and cooling ✳ Buy less stuff ✳ Use energy saving devices ✳ Switch off electricity when not in use (especially stand by lights) ✳ Use less hot water ✳ Buy locally produced foods ✳ Use warm jumpers ✳ Recycle ✳ Save forests

What is E-waste?

E-waste is made up of computers, televisions, telephones, mobile phones and electronic toys. It contains toxic chemicals such as mercury, cadmium and lead. All these devices can be recycled. Most major computer companies offer trade-ins for computers. Some companies offer pick-up and accept all computers regardless of brand. Local councils also have council clean-up days. So think twice before you throw away your e-waste.

This decorative paper is made from recycled paper.

Paper, Glass, Plastic, Steel and Aluminium

You can **recycle** all types of paper and cardboard, glass jars, plastic bottles, steel and aluminium cans in special bins collected by most councils once a week. Different councils accept different **recyclables**. Some will ask you to remove lids from bottles, some take envelopes with windows. Other councils will collect all types of plastics. See the section called 'Want to know more?' to find out what's being recycled in your area.

Glass bottles & jars

Plastic bottles

Steel cans

Aluminium cans

Recycle and Reuse

In nature everything is **recycled**. Nothing is ever wasted. But humans tend to just throw things away. Recycling saves **resources** and water and prevents all sorts of chemicals going into the water, air and land. Recycling is not just about putting the cans, plastics and cardboard out for the garbage collectors once a week. Nowadays you can recycle just about anything: mobile phone batteries, ink cartridges, computers and clothes. Remember the old saying: Waste not, want not!

Plastic Bags: Just Say No!

When you throw away a plastic bag it doesn't just disappear; it can last for as long as 1000 years! Plastic bags pollute both the land and sea, clog our waterways and kill large numbers of wildlife. It's crazy to think they are used once then chucked away. Many shops now provide paper or cloth bags, and supermarkets sell them. When you go shopping don't forget to take along your own bags!

Plastic bags kill 100 000 birds, whales, seals and turtles each year.

Recycling Tips

1. When you put materials into your recycling bin, don't put them in a plastic bag. Anything in plastic bags will end up in landfill.
2. Remove the lids from your plastic bottles and rinse them out.
3. Don't put ovenproof glass, drinking glasses or ceramic mugs in your recycling container.
4. Take cans home with you and recycle them with your other **recyclable** items.
5. Keep recycling those newspapers! Last year, Australians **recycled** over two billion newspapers, making us the world's best newspaper recyclers.
6. Metal lids can also be **recycled** if metal is accepted for recycling. Place these lids, including jam jar lids and bottle tops, inside the steel can.
7. Remove all food from containers.
8. Recycle printer cartridges. See planetark.org
9. Corks are collected through Guides Australia, or just reuse them.
10. Drop off your old mobile phones at a mobile phone shop—most have recycling bins.
11. Plastic shopping bags can be **recycled** at most supermarkets.

Recycled or Recyclable?

Both **recycled** and **recyclable** goods carry the same symbol. Words underneath the symbol will tell you whether the product is **recycled** or **recyclable**. **Recycled** products have already been **recycled**. They will have the percentage of **recycled** material listed underneath.

100% Recycled

Recyclable

Don't Shop `til you Drop!

We love to shop! Most households will have the latest TVs, DVD players and computers. If Jack next door has a new scooter, chances are you'll want one too. But do you really need it? And are there ways you can have what you want without buying it new? The answer is to be a green shopper—buy recycled, or second-hand.

This old bike has lasted well as it was made of quality materials.

Buy Quality Stuff

In the old days when things were broken, they could be fixed. Nowadays the shops are flooded with cheap items that are thrown away and easily replaced. Sadly, this is making the Earth into a rubbish heap. So when you buy things make sure they're made out of solid materials that won't break easily. And if they're recyclable all the better!

Second-hand Treasures

If you're buying a skateboard, DVDs or a bike (or just about anything!) think about doing a swap with a friend. Why not form a barter club at school? Bartering is just another word for swapping. Perhaps a friend owns something you want and you own something they want? Or sign onto one of the many swap marts now online. Thousands of members give things away every day. If there isn't a local group, you can start your own.

A bargain in a second-hand shop.

Swap 'til You Drop

Auction houses sell all sorts of stuff, like bikes, surf boards, games and dolls. And they're much cheaper than in normal shops. Then there's Ebay, an online auction house where you can bid for just about anything. You can also get second-hand things cheap at garage sales, charity shops or the recycling centre at your local tip.

Make your pocket money go further—buy second hand.

Less is More

Items with less packaging are better for the environment. Many shops (especially organic ones) now allow you to bring your own packaging. Look for products that have less chemicals and colouring. The less humans have had to do with the making of a product the better.

Excess packaging ends up at the tip, along with the other things we throw away.

Nature's Clothing

When it comes to clothing, it's a good idea to go with natural fibres. Man-made (or synthetic) fibres are often treated with very harsh chemicals that can pollute the environment. Clothes made from natural organic fibres like some cotton, hemp, linen and wool garments are better for the environment because they don't use harsh chemicals when they grow the fibres or make the clothes. Buy naturally dyed clothes if you can.

Environmentally
Friendly Food

Often farmers use chemicals to stop pests eating crops. Animals can be drenched with drugs to prevent disease. So how do you choose foods that are better for the environment? The answer is to eat organically produced foods. Avoid buying processed or packaged foods that use more energy to make and produce more waste. Buy less takeaway foods and cook your own. Eat locally grown food or start your own fruit and vegie garden.

Check for the Logo

Proper organic food is labelled 'Certified organic'. Anyone can call their product 'organic', but they can't be certified unless they've met strict standards. Certification takes several years. This gives farmers the chance to learn about organic farming and clear any chemicals from their land.

Look for the organic logo on labels.

Organic Foods

Nowadays you can buy organic fruit, vegetables, coffee and tea, cheese, meat, eggs and bread. Organic farming means crops are grown without using additives or harsh chemicals to kill pests and diseases. Organic fertilisers like animal manure and worm juice are used to feed the soil rather than man-made fertilisers. You can also buy organic meats produced with no drugs or chemicals used in the soil or the feed.

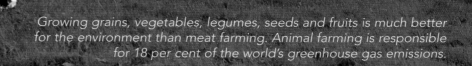

Growing grains, vegetables, legumes, seeds and fruits is much better for the environment than meat farming. Animal farming is responsible for 18 per cent of the world's greenhouse gas emissions.

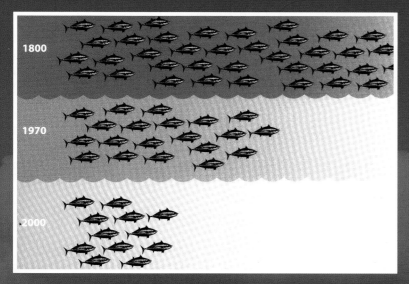

1800
1970
2000

Sustainable Seafood

Around the world, seafood is being eaten faster than it can grow. Big fish especially, such as tuna, sharks and swordfish, are in danger of becoming extinct. Avoid eating overfished species. Don't forget that by choosing organic and recycled goods you are stopping large amounts of chemicals from going into oceans and rivers. This will help fish too.

There are a lot fewer fish in the sea than there used to be.

Fresh is Best

Fresh food is better for the environment than processed food. Processing means the food goes through lots of stages before it lands on your plate. Imagine the journey of a hamburger. The ingredients and packaging have to travel to where the burger is made then machines are used to produce them, using up lots of fossil fuels. But if you grew the tomato, lettuce and cucumber yourself and made the bread and sauce, all you have to buy is the cheese and meat. Fresh food is much better for growing bodies too!

Food Miles

In the old days you could only buy a plum in summer. You might only get mangos if you lived in the tropics. Only recently have we been able to eat fruits and vegetables of all seasons all the time. This is because now we can fly food from wherever we like. So a lemon might come all the way from California. This might be practical for us, but not great news for the environment. This creates more greenhouse gases in the environment, which leads to more global warming. One way to stop this from happening is to buy local produce. Or better still, grow your own.

Grow Your Own Strawberries

Strawberries are easy to grow. Fill a terracotta pot with some potting mix. Then sprinkle with strawberry seeds or plant small plants from your local garden centre. Water well. Now just wait for the fruit to develop and eat when the fruit is ripe and red.

How Green is Your Garden?

Imagine your suburb before humans lived there. It's filled with native bushland and thousands of animals including millions of insects. Now imagine that by gardening you can put some of that ecosystem back. Every plant and animal has a right to be here—in fact we can't survive without them. Gardening makes this dream a reality. Gardening doesn't have to be something you do on your own. It can connect you with the seasons and the people around you. So go on! Get grubby!

Organic Gardening—No More Chemicals

Most bugs in the garden actually help your garden grow. Bees help to pollinate plants. Ladybeetles control aphids. Spiders eat insects that can eat your plants. So there's no need to use chemicals in the garden. When you use nasty chemicals to kill bad bugs you usually end up killing the good ones as well. Organic gardening tricks include companion planting (plants that keep away bugs) and using natural fertilisers like seaweed and worm juice.

Chickens are great in an organic garden. They will eat scraps and weeds and turn them into fertiliser. They'll also produce eggs.

Be a Water Warrior

Mulching plants with materials such as bark, straw and pebbles helps save water in the garden. Mulch around the base of plants helps prevent water evaporating. Choose drought-tolerant plants that can handle less watering. You can also use recycled 'grey' water (from the washing machine) to water your plants. Nurseries sell inexpensive devices to help make grey water okay to use in the garden. Rainwater tanks are a terrific way to recycle water. Water your garden early in the morning or at night.

Straw used as mulch can help prevent water from evaporating.

Go Native

Many native plant species will survive with little or no watering. Choose natives from your local region. You can learn about natives for free by going along to your local bush, coast or river regeneration group. These are run by most major councils. Groups get to learn about native flowers, animals and insects and how to deal with weeds.

The kangaroo paw can grow in many parts of Australia.

Composting

Set up a compost bin to change your kitchen scraps into rich soil. Get a cardboard box and dig the top flaps of the box into the ground. Open up the bottom of the box. Insert kitchen scraps like old vegies, egg shells, coffee, tea and fruit or vegie peels. In between the food scraps place shredded paper, straw and dry leaves. Every few days give it a good turn with a garden fork to put some air into it. Soon the cardboard will also break down and within a few weeks you should have some beautiful compost.

Compost bins come in all shapes and sizes.

Wonderful Worm Farms

Worm farms and worms can be bought from your local garden centre and require very little care. Worms convert your fruit and vegie scraps into rich fertiliser for your soil. Give the worms small amounts of scraps (but no onions or citrus). In a few weeks you will have castings (worm poo) to plant seedlings in, and the worm juice (worm pee) for fertiliser. Use ten parts water to one part worm juice.

Planes, Trains and Cars

What's the greenest form of transport? That's easy, it's your legs. If it's too far to walk, ride your bike. Buses, trams and trains carry a lot of people, so they would be your next option, then cars. A new type of car, the hybrid, is getting more popular each day. Travelling locally is fairly easy, but what about next time you go on a holiday overseas? Even then there are some simple rules that help to make your flight a bit greener.

Walk Against Warming

Walking is by far the best form of transport for the environment. So if you can get there easily by chucking on your sneakers, then go for it. Walking can help you stay trim and fit. It's also a great way to take in nature, breathe fresh air, spot animals and meet with neighbours and friends.

*Toyota's Prius is one of the most popular **hybrids**.*

Hybrid Cars

Most cars run on petrol, a fossil fuel, which is also one of the greatest polluters of the world today. One alternative to the petrol-only car is the hybrid car. Hybrid cars run on electricity and petrol. But you don't have to plug them in to get your power. You fill them with petrol like other cars. The system then captures energy (for example when you brake) and converts it into electricity. Plug-in hybrid cars mainly run on electricity. When their batteries run low, you plug them into the power outlet and recharge the batteries.

Peanut Anyone?

Did you know that the first cars were built to run on potato starch, corn and peanut oil? They could also use petrol (or crude oil), but eventually petrol took over as the fuel of choice because it was cheaper. Nowadays, the world uses about 83 million barrels of oil a day. Burning oil releases the greenhouse gas carbon dioxide into the atmosphere. This leads to global warming.

Buses

A full bus can keep up to 50 cars off the road each trip. That's a saving of over 1000 tonnes of greenhouse gases a year (about the weight of 200 elephants!). Nowadays, some buses are powered by gas and emit less pollution than petrol. Diesel fuel from vegetable oil or animal fats, called biodiesel, can be made from waste cooking oil and oil-seed crops to power vehicles. Hydrogen is also used to fuel all sorts of transport including buses and cars. And all you'll see coming out of a hydrogen bus is pure steam!

This Eco-bus is fuelled by hydrogen.

Up, Up and Away

Plane pollution is more harmful because it affects a far more sensitive part of the atmosphere. People can fly less often and stay longer. Did you know that flying at night is worse for the environment? Planes leave clouds in their wake. During the day these clouds help to deflect the heat from the sun but at night the clouds act like a blanket, increasing global warming. Some people who fly buy **carbon credits**. When you buy a carbon credit, that money goes into wind energy or planting trees, to make up for the pollution from your flight.

Trains and Trams

Trains and trams reduce **greenhouse gas emissions**. Provided they are nearly full, the **emissions** per passenger are small.

Bike It

Riding a bike can be great fun, and an easy way to get from one place to another. If you don't have good bike tracks in your suburb, write a letter to your local council to ask for tracks to be built. You can also start a petition at school. Some schools have started to use 'bike buses' and 'walking buses', where a group of children all ride or walk together to school.

Bioenergy

Sugar cane can be used to make ethonol fuel.

Bioenergy is renewable energy made from natural sources such as corn, oats, soybean and flax. When bioenergy is used instead of fossil fuels the amount of carbon dioxide going into the air is reduced. Bioenergy can be used for heating, to fuel certain cars and buses, to generate electricity and as a substitute for oil when making plastics. Examples of environmentally friendly fuels are ethanol, made with sugar cane, and biodiesel, produced from vegetable oils or animal fat blended with alcohol.

Answers Blowing in the Wind

Wind power is made when wind turns turbines that power an electrical generator. Due to lulls in the wind, wind power has to be supplemented by hydro or gas turbines. Location is important, with most wind farms being on hills where they can catch the wind. Wind power is the cheapest of the new renewable energy sources. Maintenance and fuel costs for wind power are almost nil but initial set-up costs can be moderately high.

Solar panels on a roof.

Turn on the Sun

The power we get from the Sun, known as solar power, can provide you with power in your home. It is usually captured by solar panels, which can be fixed on to your roof. This type of energy can provide hot water, home heating and cooling, cooking and electricity. Solar power can also help to run cars, industry and machines. Many governments hope to run whole cities on solar power.

Renewable Energy

Burning fossil fuels—coal, oil and gas—produces greenhouse gases. These are the main cause of global warming. Another problem with fossil fuels is that within 50 to 100 years most of the Earth's oil and gas will run out. There will be no more petrol to run cars, natural gas to heat houses, or crude oil to make plastics. It will be too dangerous to the Earth's climate to burn coal. Humans are going to have to find other forms of energy. This is why it is so important to explore alternative fuels. Renewable energy means using sustainable resources that will never run out, like wind, solar and wave power—we call this green power.

Geothermal Power from Hot Rocks

Rocks beneath the Earth's surface can get red hot. Geothermal power is energy generated by heat stored in those rocks. Water is pumped down one hole, turns into steam and rises up another hole. Once it reaches the surface it drives a turbine and makes electricity. Energy from geothermal power is clean and safe. The water is recycled over and over, and there are very low carbon emissions, so it is a truly sustainable energy source.

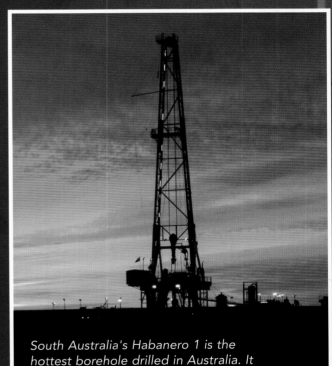

South Australia's Habanero 1 is the hottest borehole drilled in Australia. It reaches temperatures greater than 250 degrees Celsius!

Wave Power

Wave power is about harnessing the power of water out in the ocean. It is a renewable energy source and is only in its early experimental days. Wave power needs more money for research to create working models of wave power stations, especially those that can handle storms and salt water. Scientists are working out how to store wave power. They are also figuring out ways to transport the energy wave power creates to the shore.

Old-fashioned Dishwashing

You can make your own dishwashing soap, the way Grandma used to make it. Use bars of pure soap with no colour or perfume added. To prepare the soap for washing dishes put it into a pan and cover with water. Heat until the soap is dissolved, then leave to stand for several hours until cold. When you're ready to wash the dishes half-fill the sink with hot water, add a teaspoon of the pure soap, a pinch of sea salt and a dash of lemon juice. You now have a natural and effective dishwashing detergent.

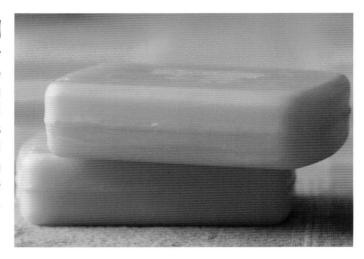

Getting Vigorous with Vinegar

Vinegar is great for killing bacteria, mould and viruses and can be used as a cleaner instead of harsh chemical sprays and powders. You can use water and a dash of vinegar to wipe down benchtops and disinfect cutting boards. For sparkling clean windows, scrunch up newspaper and put some vinegar on it; use this directly on the glass. Spray vinegar on bathroom tiles and finish with an old linen tea towel. To clean the toilet, flush it once to wet the bowl, sprinkle with bi-carbonate of soda and a dash of vinegar and scrub with a toilet brush. To clean floors, fill a quarter of a bucket with hot water, add a dash of vinegar and two drops of eucalyptus oil.

Pure and Natural Clothes Washing

Laundry detergents that contain chemicals called phosphates irritate human skin and are washed into our waterways. Natural dishwashing detergents and laundry products are now made from pure soaps, natural salts and essential oils. Instead of commercial fabric softener, use half a cup of bi-carbonate of soda. Remember also that clothes dryers use up a lot of energy. Hang clothes on the line instead.

Keeping Yourself Nice

Many shampoos, body washes, cosmetics and toothpastes contain chemicals that can cause allergic reactions, breathing problems and harm our body's ability to fight disease. Many of these harsh chemicals also harm the environment when washed into our waterways and sprayed into the air. Use locally produced organic products and make sure there are no added colours or fragrances.

Aerosols and sprays pollute our air and atmosphere.

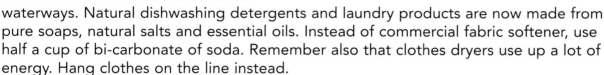

Clean **Green** Home

Go to your kitchen sink and open the cupboard door. Count the chemicals. You may find a toxic cocktail of cleaning sprays, deodorisers and detergents. Guess what? You can throw most of these things out, and replace them with natural ingredients like bicarbonate of soda, vinegar and salt. Household chemicals pollute the air and our waterways and can make people sick and irritable. There are natural ways to keep ourselves and our homes sweet smelling that won't harm the environment.

Pest-free Naturally

Fly sprays and bug killers kill all those nasties around your home, but imagine all those chemicals settling on your food, cooking utensils, toothbrush and clothing. Stay pest-free naturally by making sure all surfaces are wiped thoroughly. Fly screens on windows and sliding doors will keep unwanted insects out. Natural products like citronella ward off mossies. Hunt around for gaps in floors and walls where nasties like cockroaches come in, and seal the gaps.

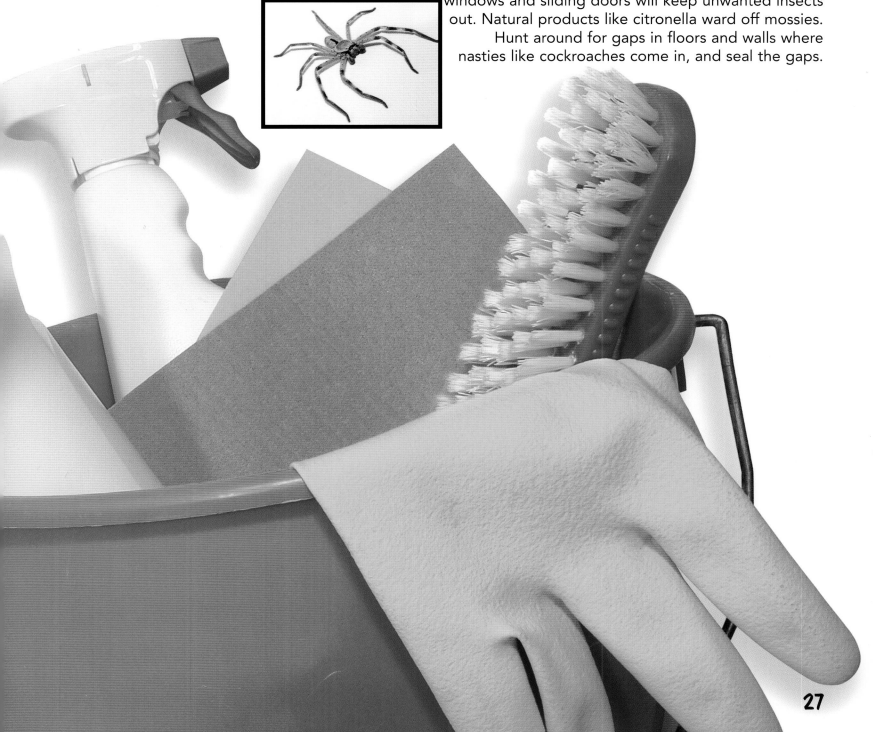

Saving Energy and Water at Home

Electrical appliances like TVs, computers and dishwashers use up a lot of electricity. So do air-conditioning and heating systems. Leaving lights on and appliances on standby (like the TV) also wastes energy. Water is so easy to get that we don't think twice when we have long showers, use the washing machine and water the garden. But we can all save water and energy at home.

Take it Easy with Water

Water-saving shower heads use less water. You can also save water by taking short three-minute showers—an egg timer can tell you when your three minutes is up. Use the half flush instead of full flush on the toilet. Washing clothes in cold water instead of hot also saves lots of energy. Rainwater tanks, underground hoses and mulching are three easy ways you can save water in the garden.

A dripping tap can waste 90 litres of water a day.

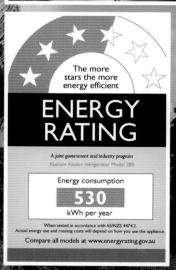

The more stars the more energy efficient

ENERGY RATING

A joint government and industry program
Kustom Kooler refrigerator Model 380

Energy consumption
530
kWh per year

When tested in accordance with AS/NZS 4474.2.
Actual energy use and running costs will depend on how you use the appliance.

Compare all models at www.energyrating.gov.au

Energy efficient appliances: the higher the star rating the more efficient the appliance and the greater savings in the long run.

Save Electricity, Money and the Environment!

Switching off power points and setting computers to sleep mode when not in use can save lots of electricity. Compact fluorescent light bulbs last up to 12 times longer than normal light bulbs and save an awful lot of energy and money, not to mention the environment. Some home appliances such as washing machines, clothes dryers, dishwashers and air-conditioners now have an energy rating label, which shows how energy efficient they are.

Keep Your Cool

The best way to stop your house from heating up is to stop the heat from getting in. If you have blinds outside the house pull them down before the day gets too hot. For some truly green protection from the heat you can also plant trees and vines outside your window. In summer you can open windows and doors instead of putting on the air conditioning. Fans in the roof can draw out hot air. Insulating batts (pink batts not vampire bats!) in the ceiling and walls stop the hot air from coming in and keep the house nice and snug in winter.

This grass roof keeps the house cool in summer and warm in winter.

Hotting Up

In winter wear an extra jumper instead of turning up the heat. You can also throw an extra blanket on the bed instead of using a heater or electric blanket. Wool blankets are a great green option as they are made from natural fibres and keep you very snug. Door snakes (material not real ones!) can also help keep out cold winter air. Heaters and air-conditioners work better when dust-free so clean them at the start of summer and winter.

If you're cold in winter put on more clothes before bumping up the heat.

Green Schools

Schools around the world are making a big difference to the environment. They are creating wonderful green spaces by planting trees, native bushland and organic gardens. Students are being taught how to monitor water and energy use, and are putting that knowledge into practice in the playground and in classrooms. Canteens are going organic and recycling, composting and worm farming are gaining popularity. Children are raising thousands of dollars to install rainwater tanks and solar panels in their schools.

Green Your Environment at School

You can start being an environmentalist by looking around your school. Are there plants in the classrooms? Are there patches of dirt in the schoolyard that could be planted with native trees? Some schools are setting up organic gardens, teaching children how to grow fruits and vegetables without chemicals. Many schools are selling only organic food from their canteens.

A student tends tomato plants.

Big Drips

Just think about all the water used in your school from taps and bubblers. Some schools have come up with new ways to deal with bubbler water that would otherwise just go down the drain. They catch the water with a pipe and use it to water the garden. Some schools have created a 'Big Drips' program, where students check bubblers and taps to help save water. Other schools raise money by door knocking and fetes to buy rainwater tanks for their school.

Solar in Schools

Some countries provide free or cheap solar panels for schools. Once panels are fitted, the school can generate some of its electricity using solar. This cuts down on greenhouse gases released through traditional coal-fired electricity and helps to limit global warming.

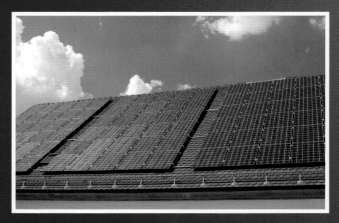

Solar panels can be fitted to a school's roof.

Recycling is Cool for School

Think about all the paper, cans of soft drink and plastic you use at school. Does your school have recycling bins? If you don't have enough bins the local council can deliver them usually for free. To recycle your food waste set up some compost bins. Worm farms are also a great way to recycle food scraps.

Bright Sparks

Some schools now have 'Bright Sparks' programs that encourage kids to check lights and fans are off when they're not needed. Remember to always switch computers and screens off when you leave the classroom. Or if you are leaving for a short time switch them to power-saving mode. Programs now exist that automatically switch appliances and computers off if they aren't being used. But if you don't have these programs you'll just have to do it the old-fashioned way—use your finger!

CHANGE FOR THE BETTER WITH ENERGY STAR

Some new computers, printers, faxes or photocopiers come with an energy star rating. An energy star appliance will switch itself into power-saving mode when not being used.

Join Green Communities

Schools are joining with environmental organisations such as Reefwatch, Streamwatch, Waterwise and Greenfleet to help save the planet. Landcare has school programs that can be adapted to your local area, whether it be seascape, arid region or urban. Eco-schools International is a program that promotes sustainable principles in schools across the world. Schools learn how to figure out what environmental issues they face and how to plan projects.

Kids join forces with Landcare to plant trees.

Organic Farming Anyone?

Did you know that you can learn to be an organic farmer during your holidays? You can feed the chickens, milk goats, plant tomatoes, learn about composting and how to pick grapes. Many places offer meals and accommodation in exchange for such work. There's even an international organisation called WWOOFs (Willing Workers on Organic Farms) that will help you organise the trip.

Eco-adventures

On an eco-adventure you travel and explore without harming the natural environment. If your family likes walking you can trek the mountains of Transylvania; sail along the river Nile in traditional Egyptian sailboats; or help restore the native habitat of the rare creatures of the Galapagos islands like the giant tortoise, sea lions and penguins. Travel agencies that care about the environment will help ensure you're getting a true green holiday.

You can help restore the habitat of the Galapagos islands' giant tortoise.

Eco-Lodges

When you go to an eco-lodge you can live like a monkey perched high in a rainforest retreat, or under the ground in a desert cave. Many eco-lodges and resorts try to preserve their natural environment; they plant trees and conduct wildlife surveys. The experience can vary depending on where you go. In Canada you can trek across a glacier. In Costa Rica you can follow the trail of a sloth. In Ecuador you can learn the ancient forest traditions of the Achuar people.

The Daintree Eco Lodge and Spa is set high in the canopy of the rainforest.

Sustainable Travel

Did you know you can have a holiday that's good for the environment? You can take an eco-holiday, have a working holiday on an organic farm, help restore an ancient rainforest, or simply go on a camping trip. Buying goods from local businesses while you're away is also good eco-tourism.

Riding is so much more fun than driving. Plus you get to see heaps more when you're not speeding past in your car!

Planning Your Trip

Before you go make sure you turn off all the stand-by lights on appliances. Make sure the hot water heater is switched off. When you're planning your holiday the best thing you can do for the environment is to go somewhere local. That way you don't use up lots of fossil fuels getting to your holiday destination (this means less global warming). But if you must fly it is better to fly during the day, than at night. Once you get there see the sights on a bike or use public transport.

Camping: The Ultimate Eco-holiday

What type of holiday uses no electricity, the only air-conditioning is the fresh breeze and the only transport is a paddle, pedals or your feet? That's right, it's camping. Camping is the ultimate eco-holiday. Pitch your tent, build a fire and rough it for a while. Just make sure you take your rubbish and recycling home with you. Take only pictures and leave only footprints.

Think Global, Act Local

Part of becoming an **environmentalist** is caring for the world around you. But it also means you care for communities other than your own. All our communities need to be environmentally sustainable if this planet is to have a chance. We can work together to protect and restore the local environment, and use less energy by building cycle paths, working close to home and buying local food, products and services. We can create community gardens, share cars and swap goods and services.

Crystal Waters Village won the 1996 World Habitat Award for its 'pioneering work in demonstrating new ways of low impact, sustainable living'. Today it accommodates about 200 people, many businesses and multiple gardens and farms.

Eco-communities

Some communities around the world try to work on sustainable principles. People create a community where humans can live harmoniously with nature, caring for the native flora and fauna. They usually design the community with bushland, community areas and work and home life close together. Farming areas are set up with bushland in harmony rather than competition. They use few pesticides and fertilisers, so native species thrive. People within the community can swap goods and services.

Community Gardens

If you don't have a garden or a balcony you can still get your hands dirty. Organic community gardens are popping up all over the world. These are gardens run by community groups in local areas. Free classes are usually held on **permaculture** principles, composting, worm farming and garden construction. Members often get to work on community areas, and their own plots. They then get to share in the wonderful organic produce that springs to life. All you need to do is ring up your local council and find out if there's a community garden in your area.

This community organic garden is being built by volunteers.

Clean Up Australia Day

There are hundreds of green events every year, but Clean Up Australia Day is one of the biggest. On this day, kids (and adults) from around Australia get together to clean up beaches, towns and parks. But don't wait till Clean Up Australia Day. Make every day a clean one. Whenever you see some rubbish put it in the rubbish bin or recycling bin. That's the wonderful thing about being a greenie: you can be one every day!

Clean Up volunteers pick up rubbish by the side of the road.

One Well at a Time

Six-year-old Ryan saw parents and children in Africa who were in desperate need of water. He wanted to buy them a well. So with the help of his whole community he raised enough money for a well. He is now 10 and has raised over $70 000 and funded many wells and schools in African communities.

Urban Area Restoration

This was the street before the Sustainable South Bronx plan was put into action. The main picture on this page shows the planned 'greening' of the street.

Sustainable South Bronx is a group of people in the United States who got together to make their urban environment a much more pleasant (and safer) place to live. They deal with issues of urban poverty, unemployment, land use, energy, transportation, water and waste policy and education. The group creates pedestrian and cycling tracks, parks and healthier waterways, and promotes recycling. They have a vision, and together they are making their small part of the Earth better.

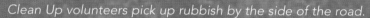

Greening Your Gifts

Gifts are a great way to show you care about someone, especially during special times like birthdays, Christmas and Mother's Day. But how can you give things and still care for the Earth? Next time you're about to buy a gift, ask yourself honestly, does this person need more stuff? Instead of buying more things, use your creative mind and make or recycle a gift. You can also donate money or a gift to a person in need and transform someone's life.

Make Your Own Cards

Instead of buying cards, how about recycling last year's cards? All you need is some scissors, recycled cardboard, old cards and magazines, and glue. Grab your old Christmas or birthday cards from last year and cut out your favourite pictures. You can also use buttons, beads, advertising from your letterbox and old material. Now get creative and design your new cards by sticking the recycled materials onto folded card. You'll have some truly eco-friendly cards that are absolutely unique!

Nature's Gifts

A thoughtful, environmentally friendly gift is fruits and vegies or flowers you have grown yourself. Put them into a lovely big basket with a recycled bow and the person will know that you haven't just bought something from the corner store. Bulbs, seeds or plants from your garden or local nursery are also beautiful gifts. Your friends will remember their present well into the year as they see it bloom before their eyes.

Home-grown bulbs make a wonderful gift.

Planet-friendly Presents

Nowadays you can buy all sorts of planet-friendly products such as organic foods, coffee and teas, or items like handmade journals, toys and musical instruments made by people from poorer nations. Organisations like Oxfam and Ten Thousand Villages, which help fight poverty, sell handmade gifts made by people around the world through their online catalogues. Or you can buy t-shirts from the Wilderness Society or Greenpeace.

Friends in Need

You can now buy gifts for people in poor nations through organisations like World Vision and Oxfam. These include things that truly make a difference in their lives like clean water, mosquito nets, wells, goats, cows and chickens! You can also donate money for micro loans. These are small loans given to people in poorer nations to help them start up a business. Imagine giving someone the gift of being able to care for themselves.

This little girl loves her goat because it provides her with milk to drink and helps her family earn extra income. (Image provided courtesy of World Vision Australia © 2007.)

World Governments
Leading the Way

We can all help to protect the environment as individuals. But governments also have to make policies that plan for the future of our Earth. Governments are supposed to represent the people: you and me. So if this isn't happening where you live, there are things you can do to make your voice heard.

Toxic Chemicals: Europe

The European Union has recently passed a law called REACH that requires companies to provide safety data on chemical products. This means that in some cases dangerous chemicals will need to be replaced with safer ones.

Greenhouse Gases: United Nations

The Kyoto Protocol created policies to help governments manage climate change. Kyoto created an international carbon market. This means that companies could buy and sell carbon credits. If a company is damaging the environment, it can pay money to companies that invest in green enterprises such as wind farms, organic farms and forests. The goal of Kyoto is to help countries reduce greenhouse emissions.

This is the flag of the United Nations; an organisation of countries that works for international peace and cooperation.

Legal Rights to Ecosystems: USA

A little town in Pennsylvania has passed a law giving ecosystems legal rights. Of course trees can't go to court, so the law states that any resident can file a lawsuit on behalf of the local ecosystem. Trees are now suing developers!

Compact Fluorescent Light Bulbs: Australia

The Australian government is the first in the world to phase out **incandescent** lamps. Compact fluorescent light bulbs are now used instead. They use less energy and have a longer life than normal light bulbs.

Carbon Neutral: New Zealand

New Zealand is set to be carbon neutral by 2020. It is phasing out its coal-mining industry and turning to green electricity.

By phasing out its polluting industries New Zealand is actively working to save its natural environment. The Routeburn Walk in New Zealand is part of the Great Walks of New Zealand.

Recycling: Europe

Companies across Europe must now pay for the collection, treatment and recovery of anything from mobile phones, toasters, refrigerators and TV sets. New laws ban four heavy metals (lead, cadmium, mercury and hexavalent chromium) as well as two groups of flame retardants. These materials were widely used in the past. Countries that supply goods to Europe must follow the new standards, which is leading to a green revolution across the world.

Pushing for Change

For local environmental issues, start by ringing your local council, writing them a letter or creating a petition. You can write to both State and federal members. The more people you can get involved the better so find out what groups are fighting for the same issue. You can also contact the media. Start with your local paper, then try city and national papers, and current affairs programs on television and radio.

Members of an environment group dress up as native animals to campaign for change on the street.

Back to the **Future**

Sometimes, it's up to us to imagine a better future. At other times, nature does it for us. All we have to do is look closely. Many of the things shown here would have been unimaginable just 10 years ago. Green living is taught in schools and at home. People are starting to consider the wealth and health of the planet over the wealth and health of themselves and their own country. Today, we are well on our way to a greener, better future.

Grin Grin is an island city in Japan. Architect Toyo Ito designed the buildings to meld with their natural environment.

Plants grow inside the buildings at Grin Grin, shown above.

Sustainable Cities

Once upon a time, cities and towns were self-sufficient. Food was grown locally for residents and suppliers were close by. Nowadays our food often travels from far away and many people drive long distances to work. City planners are now designing future cities with the past in mind so that people don't have to travel far to work and play. Architects are designing buildings using natural power, heating, cooling and ventilation. Governments are passing new laws that support sustainable design. Organic city farms are now supplying food to locals.

Renewable Energy

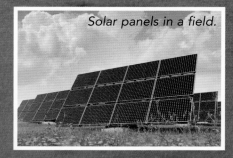

Solar panels in a field.

People are buying green power, made using renewable energy like wind and solar. This makes energy companies look for more green options. Governments are putting money into sustainable energy solutions. They will consider the resources available such as ample sunlight, wave and wind power.

Green Corridors and Gardens

People are starting to see how important plants are for the environment and humans. From cities to country towns, bush regeneration sites and gardens link up like one giant nature strip. Native plants and animals can now get from place to place.

With over 200 different species of plants on its walls, the Museum of Quai Branly is helping to green a major city, Paris.

Using Water Wisely

People recycle water in their gardens and homes and collect water in rain tanks. With the planting of new native trees holding down the soil, the natural water cycle is being restored to its healthy state. Governments are starting to encourage long-term sustainable water solutions.

The Sturt Desert Pea will survive in the driest regions. Many Australian natives need little water.

Paying for Pollution

In some countries taxes are being placed on pollution, making it too expensive to pollute the environment. People the world over are becoming more aware of what they throw away and are using natural rather than man-made products. More businesses are making products from natural materials. Soon we will be able to buy musical instruments, jewellery, plant pots, bowls, vases, furniture, lamps and much more; all made from natural, biodegradable materials.

Old-fashioned Farming

Farmers are rediscovering traditional ways of farming that work with nature rather than against it. They find what crops are best for different types of land and learn how to manage water better. The soil is enriched rather than degraded. Natural fertilisers and ways of controlling pests and diseases are being investigated. More people are buying organic and free-range foods.

Activities
The Environment Quiz

1. List three important reasons why we need to care for our environment. (Pages 6–7)

2. Pick either a plant, animal, insect, fungi or human. Draw a picture of how it relies on other things on this page to live. (Pages 8–9)

3. Name three types of pollution and what we can do about it. (Pages 10–11)

4. What things can you do to help stop climate change? (Pages 12–13)

5. Name the four types of recycling bins on this page and what goes in them. (Pages 14–15)

6. Name three examples of natural organic fibres. (Pages 16–17)

7. Why is it better to buy organic than non-organic foods? (Pages 18–19)

8. Name three ways to save water in the garden. (Pages 20–21)

9. What is the best form of transport for the environment? (Pages 22-23)

10. Why is renewable energy better for the planet? (Pages 24–25)

11. What kinds of chemicals do you use in your home? What environmentally friendly products can you replace them with? (Pages 26–27)

12. List three ways to keep your home cool in summer, without using an air conditioner. (Pages 28–29)

13. What things can you do in your school to save water and energy? (Pages 30–31)

14. Where could you go for an environmentally friendly holiday? (Pages 32–33)

15. What sorts of things are people doing to make cities better places to live in? (Pages 34–35)

16. How can giving a goat to a family in need, help that family and the community? (Pages 36–37)

17. Pick a world government from this page and explain what they are doing to make this world a greener place. (Pages 38–39)

18. What are architects doing to make more environmentally friendly buildings? (Pages 40–41)

Things to Do

1. Go around the house and garden and find five different ways that you use water in your life.

2. Find an example of a food chain in your garden. Draw it.

3. How is our natural environment thrown out of balance by humans? Walk around your neighbourhood and find examples there.

4. Research the ways climate change will effect your part of the world. Will it get hotter? Will it get more rain? What will happen to the plants and animals?

5. Go to your local shops and try to find as many goods made from recycled materials as you can. Have a competition with your friends to see who can find the most second-hand goods.

6. Set up a swapping group at school.

7. Go to your local supermarket and find three types of organic foods. Were they easy to find? List them here.

8. Research what plants once lived in your area. You can visit your local national park. Or make an excursion to a nearby bush regeneration site. Use these plants as a guide to what you should plant in your garden or school.

9. Create a model of the perfect environmental transport vehicle. What does it run on? How many people fit into it? What waste comes out of it, if any?

10. Make a kite out of paper, ribbon and some string. When you fly that kite you are harnessing the power of the wind!

11. Work your way around the house finding gaps and cracks where critters can get in. Help parents seal up those cracks.

12. Participate in the 40-hour drought. This means you use only 40 litres of water in 40 hours. It is harder than you think!

13. Set up a Bright Sparks or Big Drips group at your school. Monitor electricity and water use. Make suggestions for savings in both these areas.

14. Set up a tent in your back yard. See what electrical stuff (like hairdryers, and TVs) you can go without for one day.

15. Check out your neighbourhood. What green projects are taking place?

16. Make a card or gift using old cards and magazines.

17. Write a story about a futuristic world where all the Earth's systems are balanced. How do all people have enough food and water to live? How do people get to places? Where do they work?

Glossary (what words mean)

Algae	groups of small marine creatures.
Antibiotics	medicine that kills bacteria. Often man-made.
Appliances	fridges, stoves, dishwashers and other household items.
Barter	swap goods for other goods, not money.
Biodegradable	will break down very easily into a natural substance.
Biodiversity	the variety of life on Earth, including all animals, plants and organisms and the places where they live.
Carbon dioxide	one of the greenhouses gases. It is necessary for life on Earth to survive.
Carbon credits	something you buy to make up for polluting the environment. The money from carbon credits goes into planting trees and conserving nature.
Carbon footprint	the amount of carbon dioxide you put out into the environment during daily activities like catching the bus and watching TV.
Carbon neutral	to produce no carbon emissions, or to produce carbon emissions and offset them (by buying carbon credits).
Climate change	a shift in the climate due to the release of greenhouse gases into the Earth's atmosphere.
Curriculum	the subjects taught in a school.
Developing country	a country with widespread poverty, and low incomes.
Ecosystems	are made up of plants and animals and the way they rely on each other and work together.
Emissions	something discharged into the air, usually a type of pollution.
Endangered	there are very few of its kind left.
Environmentalist	someone who works to save the environment.
Extinct	the species is wiped out and none of its kind are left.
Fertiliser	organic (e.g. animal manure and seaweed) and inorganic forms (e.g. ammonia) and is used to make a plant grow.
Fossil fuel	fuels formed by minerals, or dead animals or plants. Refer to oil, coal, petrol and natural gas, which are now in limited supply and usually major polluters.
Glacier	a mass of ice that moves very slowly.
Global warming	the heating of the Earth, due mostly to human activities, but can also occur naturally.

Greenhouse gases include carbon dioxide, methane, nitrous oxide, water vapour and ozone. Some of these are produced by humans, but others occur naturally. Too many of certain greenhouse gases can contribute to global warming.

Grey water is the water left over after you wash your clothes. Sometimes it needs to be treated before it can be used in the garden.

Herbicide harsh chemical used to kill plants or weeds.

Hybrid cars that run on electricity and petrol. It can also mean a mixing of two different things.

Incandescent light bulbs a type of light bulb that uses a great deal of energy. These are being replaced in some countries by more energy efficient light bulbs.

Indigenous come from the local area.

Mulch covers the soil and lessens water evaporation. Can come in lots of forms including tree bark, wood chips, newspaper, straw, sawdust as well as man-made things like plastic. It saves water in the garden.

Non-renewable resources things which will run out like coal, petroleum and natural gas.

Organic in this book means made without harsh chemicals, such as hormones, antibiotics and synthetic products.

Ozone layer particles of the gas ozone in the Earth's atmosphere that protect the Earth from the sun's rays.

Permaculture is about working with nature to create sustainable systems. It is used in agriculture, building and design.

Pesticides chemicals used to kill pests.

Petition a letter with names and signatures on it. Usually sent to a company or government to try to make them change what they are doing.

Pollinate to help fertilise a plant with pollen. Bees and other bugs do this by flying from plant to plant.

Rebate money given by government, to people who buy certain environmentally friendly goods (like solar panels).

Recyclable means it can be recycled.

Recycled means it has already been recycled.

Renewable resources things which can be re-grown, or which will last the Earth's lifetime.

Sustainable to live in an environmentally friendly way making sure the Earth's things last and don't run out.

Want to Know More?

Following are websites where you can find out more about the environment and learn how to help make the world a better place.

Australian Sustainable Schools Initiative (AuSSI) (http://www.environment.gov.au/education/aussi) is about helping create sustainable schools.

Alternative Technology Association (ATA) (http://www.ata.org.au/) information on solar panels, biofuels, wind technology and lots more.

Australian Marine Conservation Society (http://www.amcs.org.au) helps you decide what seafood is ok to eat.

Carbon Footprint (http://www.carbonfootprint.com) helps you calculate your carbon footprint.

Care2 (http://www.care2.com) a network of people from around the world interested in green living.

Clean Up Australia Day (http://www.cleanup.com.au) tells you when this event is on and what you can do.

Clean Up the World (http://www.cleanuptheworld.org/en/) tells you how to organise a clean up day.

Community Gardens Network (http://www.communitygarden.org.au) has plenty of tips on starting up a community garden.

Compact groups (http://groups.yahoo.com/group/thecompact) promise to stop buying non-essential things.

CSIRO Scientriffic (http://www.csiro.au/resources/ScientrifficMain.html) is a science magazine for ages seven and up.

Earth 911 (http://earth911.org/just-for-kids/) is a site for kids about the environment.

Eco Schools International (http://www.eco-schools.org) is a site with step-by-step guides for schools wanting to make environmental changes.

Energy Allstars (http://energyallstars.gov.au) helps you compare energy efficient appliances.

Fair trade (http://www.fairtrade.net) teaches you about fair trade with developing nations.

Freecycle (http://www.freecycle.org) is a free worldwide online community where people give away things they don't want.

Greenhouse Office (http://www.greenhouse.gov.au/yourhome/technical/index.htm) offers a home manual for energy saving.

Greenroofs (http://www.greenroofs.com) tells you all about green roofs.

Kids Create Your Future (http://www.kidsforfuture.net) is a website for children who want to make a better future.

Landcare (http://www.landcareonline.com/) shows you how you can join groups that care for bush, urban land, rivers and coasts.

Nabuur (http://www.nabuur.com) is an organisation that helps volunteers link up through their computers to communities in need.

Oxfam (http://www.oxfamunwrapped.com.au) gifts for people in need.

Planet Ark (http://www.planetark.org) to find out about National Plant a Tree Day and recycling.

Planet Patrol (http://www.planetpatrol.info) is a green website made for kids by kids.

Recycling Near You (http://www.recyclingnearyou.com.au) to find information on recycling in your local area.

Save Water (http://www.savewater.com.au) shows you how to save water.

Solar Schools (http://www.solarschools.net/) is the National Solar Schools Educational Website.

Sustainable South Bronx (http://www.ssbx.org/) shows amazing examples of urban area environmental work.

Tools for Healthy Schools (http://www.netspeed.com.au/rdi/cas/tfhs/index.html) looks out for toxic chemicals in schools.

TravelSmart (http://www.travelsmart.gov.au) for information on bike plans, green transport and 'walking buses'.

Water Can (http://www.watercan.com) works to provide clean water to poor communities.

Water Footprint of Nations (http://www.waterfootprint.org) shows you how much water each country uses.

World Vision (http://www.worldvision.com.au/Smiles/GiftCatalogue/Default.aspx) contains gifts for people in poorer nations, like goats.

World Wildlife Fund (http://www.wwf.org) allows you to adopt an endangered animal.

WWOOFs (Willing Workers on Organic Farms) (http://www.wwoof.org) tells you how to volunteer on an organic farm.

Index

Remember the 3 Rs for the environment in order

Reduce   consumption of raw materials and energy.
Re-use   what you can or pass it on to someone else who needs it.
Recycle   everything else.

First published in Australia in 2008 by Young Reed
an imprint of New Holland Publishers (Australia) Pty Ltd
Sydney o Auckland o London o Cape Town

1/66 Gibbes St Chatswood NSW 2067 Australia
218 Lake Road Northcote Auckland 0627 New Zealand
86 Edgware Road London W2 2EA United Kingdom
80 McKenzie Street Cape Town 8001 South Africa

National Library of Australia Cataloguing-in-Publication Data:

Perini, Jessica.

Environment: Saving Our Planet/author, Jessica Perini.
Chatswood, NSW. New Holland Publishers, 2008.

ISBN: 9781921073502 (hbk.) For primary school age.

A823.4

Commissioning Editor: Yani Silvana
Editor: Jenny Scepanovic
Designer: Tania Gomes
Production Manager: Linda Bottari
Printer: Tien Wah Press, Malaysia

Picture credits

Abbreviations: t = top, b = bottom, l = left,
r = right, c = centre, bg = background

AAD: p12tl
Australian Certified Organic: p. 18c
Australian Greenhouse Office: p. 28bl; p. 31c
Australian Marine Conservation Society: p. 19tl
Clean Up Australia: p. 35c
Crystal Waters Village: p. 34tl
Daintree Eco Lodge & Spa: p. 32bl
Department for Planning and Infrastructure,
Western Australia: p. 23tr
Geodynamics Limited: p. 25cr
Gilbert Gamolo: p. 11tr
Ian Faulkner: p13cr
Jean-Christophe Froissard: p. 39c; p. 41tl; p.41tr
Landcare Australia: p. 31bl
Daryl Morris, The Wilderness Society: p. 39bl
Matthew Morrison: pp. 10-11bg; pp. 12–13bg;
  p. 38c
NASA: p. 7bg; 12c; 12bl
NSW Department of Environment and Climate
Change (DECC): p. 14br; p. 15br
Jessica Perini: cover; p. 1; pp. 2-3; pp. 4-5; p. 9c;
p.9br; pp. 14-15bg; p. 14c; p. 17tr; p. 19c; p. 19bl;
p. 21tl; p. 21tr; p. 21cr; pp. 22-23bg; p. 23br; p.
26tr; p. 26c; p. 26br; p. 28c; p. 30c; p. 35tl; p. 36c;
p. 41br; p. 48bg
Michael Perini: pp. 32-33bg; p. 33br; pp. 44-45bg;
  pp. 46-47
Ron Prendergast, Melbourne Zoo: p. 15c
Chie Rokutanda: pp. 40-41bg; p. 40bl
Sims E-Recycling: p. 14tl
Sustainable South Bronx: pp. 34-35bg; p. 35br
Sydney City Toyota: p. 22c
Todd Sowers, LDEO, Columbia University: p. 12tr
Roaring 40s: p. 1; pp. 24-25bg
Roy Wangsa: p. 11c
World Vision: pp. 37bg
All other images Istock